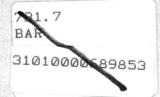

ART OF THE TOTEM

Totem Poles
of the
Northwest Coastal Indians

by
Marius Barbeau

ISBN 0-88839-168-4
Copyright © 1984 Marius Barbeau

Catalog in Publication Data

Barbeau, Marius, 1883-1969.
Art of the totem

Revision, with added ill., of an article printed by the U.S.
Government Printing Office in 1932.
    Includes index.
    ISBN 0-88839-168-4

    1. Totem poles — Northwest coast of North America. 2.
Indians of North America — Northwest coast of North
America. — Art. I. Title.
II. Title: Totem Poles: A Recent Native Art of the Northwest
Coast of America.
E78.N78B37   732'.2'09795   C83-091106-5

Edited by Susan Gillis, Diana Ottosen
Typeset by Elizabeth Grant in Times Roman
    on an AM Varityper Comp/Edit
Production, Layout & Cover Design by Crystal Ryan
Printed in Canada by Friesen Printers

Hancock House Publishers Ltd.
19313 Zero Avenue, Surrey, B.C. V3S 5J9

Hancock House Publishers Inc.
1431 Harrison Avenue, Blaine, Wash., U.S.A. 98230

CONTENTS

INTRODUCTION

The text of this book was originally published as *Totem Poles: A Recent Native Art of the Northwest Coast of America* by the United States Government Printing Office in 1932. It has been reorganized and updated, and many new photographs have been added to those of the author, anthropologist Marius Barbeau.

The totem poles of British Columbia and Alaska on the northwest coast of North America are famous throughout the world. Their decorative style at its best is a unique form of aboriginal art. Impressive and intriguing, the totems express native personality and craftsmanship. Museums of Europe, Canada, and America treasure a number of totem poles, the majority from the Queen Charlotte Islands. Totems also adorn the parks of cities along the Northwest Coast. These picturesque creations, however, can be seen to full advantage only in their true home at the edge of the ocean, amid tall cedars and hemlocks, in the shadow of lofty mountains. Their bold profiles stand starkly against their surroundings of luxuriant dark green vegetation, under skies of bluish mist.

Few totems are found in their original surroundings, however. Many have fallen from old age, have decayed, or simply disappeared. Some were sold; others were removed without the consent or knowledge of their owners. Quite a few were destroyed by the Indians themselves, during hysterical Christian revivals. For instance, the poles of two Tsimshian tribes, which once stood at Gitlarhdamks and Port Simpson, near the Alaskan frontier, were destroyed in the winters of 1917 and 1918.

Kwakiutl house and free standing pole.
B.C. Archives

4

SIGNIFICANCE

The characteristic figures on totem poles are symbols comparable to family crests, not images of pagan gods or demons, as is often supposed. They usually illustrate myths or tribal traditions. Poles were not worshipped; if they were held sacred it was only because of the historic significance of the carved figures.

The totems of the Tsimshian and the Tlingit in particular, as well as many Haida poles, were erected by various families in the tribe as monuments to the dead, serving the same purpose as our tombstones. In fact, native crests carved in stone or marble were sometimes used as tombstones in several graveyards in Port Simpson and Vancouver.

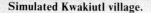

Simulated Kwakiutl village.

The owners displayed their crests on a totem pole to establish and make public their claims to vested rights and privileges. The emblems or totems varied with each family; they were exclusive property and were jealously guarded. They depicted legends, events, and the animals of the country. The eagle, raven, frog, finback whale, grizzly bear, wolf, mythical thunderbird, and many other animals occur frequently on poles. Others less frequently seen appear to be more recent traditions: the owl, salmon, woodpecker, beaver, starfish, shark, halibut, bullhead, split person, mountain goat, puma, moon, stars, and the rainbow.

Milwaukee Public Museum

7

The legendary origin of each crest was explained in traditional narratives that were recited at winter festivals or potlatches. These stories told of the adventures of ancestors; how they were harassed or rescued by spirits and monsters of the unseen regions; how benevolent spirits appeared in visions and invested their protégés with charms; and how ancient warriors conquered their enemies. The carved illustrations of these stories served a definite purpose. Besides commemorating the dead and establishing ownership, they familiarized youths with legends of their past, keeping that part of their heritage alive.

Shortly after the death of a chief, his prospective heirs appointed his leading nephew to his post. The new chief's induction took place in the midst of a large number of invited guests during an elaborate festival or potlatch. The name of the uncle passed on to his nephew, and the erection of a totem pole crowned the event. Groups of related families mustered all available resources to make the feast as lavish as possible, as their standing and influence depended on a display of generosity.

National Museum of Canada

Tlingit pole at Saxman village Alaska.

Bella Coola pole.
National Museum of Canada

◀
Tsimshian pole figure.
B.C. Dept. Travel

9

The process of making a totem pole — of cutting a large red cedar tree, hauling it overland or on the sea for a considerable distance, carving it, and erecting it — often took years. A tree was first selected and felled by people who were not members of the family which had commissioned the work. These people were fed and paid publicly once the tree had been felled. A carver was then hired from among the families who had commissioned the felling. Should he lack the required skill, it was his privilege to appoint a substitute over whom he stood ceremonially, assuming the credit for the work. The carving was accomplished as secretly as possible, the figures being selected by the owners from the list of available family crests, which might number more than five.

At the completion of the carving, when enough food and wealth had been amassed for the erection of a pole, invitations were sent to all the leading families of the neighboring tribes. The pole was erected with the help of hundreds of people gathered for the festivities that were the cornerstone of social life until the late 1890s.

These carved memorials generally faced the shores of rivers or the ocean — the coastal Indians' main highways. They stood apart from one another in front of the owners' houses, and dotted the whole length of a village in an irregular line. As villages were moved to new locations, the poles were left behind in the deserted sites. Trees grew up around them in several places, making them difficult to find today.

ERECTING A POLE

Inside house post.
National Museum of Canada

Kwakuitl pole showing crests (top to bottom): Eagle, Thunderbird, and Bear.
Field Museum of Natural History, Chicago

11

Hand adzes with stone blades.

Mongo Martin Memorial Pole being raised at Alert Bay, B.C.
B.C. Govt. Photo

DEVELOPMENT

The art of carving and erecting memorial columns is not really as ancient on the Northwest Coast as is generally believed. Popular misconceptions that surviving totem poles are hundreds of years old are proven false by the nature of the materials and the climatic conditions of this region. A green cedar cannot stand upright much longer than fifty or sixty years on the upper Skeena, where precipitation is moderate and the soil consists of gravel and sand. Along the coast, only a few still stand today that were erected over a century ago. The intense moisture that prevails most of the year and the muskeg foundation aid the decaying process. The totem poles of Port Simpson, for instance, all decayed on the south side first, the side exposed to warm, rainy winds. Most of the well-known poles found in parks and museums were carved after 1860, while several of those remaining in Indian villages, such as Alert Bay, were erected much later.

The flourishing of native carving techniques was largely confined to the nineteenth century. It hinged upon European tools — the steel axe, the adze, and the curved knife — which were traded off in large numbers to the natives after contact, in 1778. The lack of suitable tools, of wealth, and of leisure time in the pre-Contact period prevented elaborate or ambitious carving projects. The material benefits arising from the fur trade stirred up jealousies and rivalries, and incited incredible efforts for higher prestige and position. The totem pole came into fashion after 1830; its size, and the beauty of its figures were a means of publicly displaying wealth and status.

At times, feuds over the size of poles broke out between semi-independent leaders within a village. One example was the bitter quarrel between *Hladerh* and *Sispegoot,* which occurred on the Nass River around 1870. *Hladerh,* head chief of the Wolves, would not allow the erection of any pole that exceeded his own in height. *Sispegoot,* head chief of the Finback Whales, could afford to disregard his rival's jealousy. When his new pole was carved, the news went out that it would be the tallest in the village. In spite of *Hladerh's* repeated warnings, *Sispegoot* issued invitations for its erection. When he was shot and wounded by *Hladerh* as he passed in front of his house in a canoe, the festival had to be postponed for a year. Meanwhile, *Hladerh* managed, through a clever plot, to have *Sispegoot* murdered by one of his own subordinates. He later compelled another chief of his own phratry, much to his humiliation, to shorten his pole twice after it was erected. His dominance was effectively checked only when he tried to spread his rule abroad to an upper Nass village.

Most of the poles of the upper Skeena were erected after 1880. Although the oldest five or six may have been erected as early as the 1860s, it is safe to say that this feature of native life among the Gitksan became fashionable only between 1870 and 1880. Only six out of nearly thirty poles at Gitwinlkul — the earliest of these villages to adopt pole carving — were erected prior to the 1880s, and only a few poles stood in the neighboring villages at that time.

The Coast Salish did not carve large poles but restricted poles to small free standing "figures" or pole-like decorations on the outside of longhouses.
National Museum of Canada

Three beautiful Tsimshian poles at Kitwanga B.C.
National Museum of Canada

Fine quality Tsimshian pole at Kitwancool leans ominously over a more modern grave memorial house.
Donovan Clemson

Native accounts and the evidence of the carved memorials lead to the conclusion that, among the Tsimshian carved house-front poles and house-corner posts were introduced first, many years before the first detached columns appeared. Several houses and posts of this kind have been described, and a few were observed, particularly at the lower canyon of the Skeena, although most of them were in an advanced state of decay.

The archaic style of house decoration was abandoned as soon as the natives gave up building large communal lodges in the traditional style. Memorial columns that could no longer serve as ceremonial doorways became the new fashion. Some of the upper Skeena villages, however, never adopted this new, free-standing style of decoration. At least four villages had no more than a few poles, and some of these were put up only after 1890.

Carving techniques on several of the oldest poles on the upper Skeena reveal earlier stages of the art. It grew out of the techniques used to make masks or to carve small detached objects. The carving on these poles represented masked and costumed performers as they appeared in festivals, rather than the real animals or objects as they existed in nature. These early Skeena River carvers had not yet acquired the skill of the Nass River masters, who had advanced to the point of thinking of a large pole as an architectural unit that called for harmony in decorative treatment.

Two master pole carvers, *Haesem-hliyawn* and *Hlamee*, of Gitwinlkul, represent distinctive periods of the craft among the Gitksan. To *Haesem-hliyawn* goes the credit of carving some of the best poles in existence. He was alive as late as 1868, while *Hlamee*, his junior and follower, died after 1900.

ITS EVOLUTION

National Museum of Canada

Tsimshian village of Kispiox.

19

The style of *Haesem-hliyawn* was one of the finest; one which was purely native. He combined a keen sense of realism with a fondness for decorative treatment. His art sought inspiration in nature, while maintaining itself within the frontiers of ancient stylistic technique. *Haesem-hliyawn* belonged to a generation which witnessed the growth and peak of totem pole art, between 1840 and 1880. His handling of human figures ranks among the outstanding achievements of native art. The faces he carved, with their exaggerated expression and amusing contortions, are characteristic of Northwest Coast art.

Hlamee, a prolific worker, introduced the white man's paint to enhance the features of his carvings. While he used paint with discretion and to good effect, it immediately lessened the sculptural quality of the work. The new fashion did not compensate for the evident loss of native inspiration and artistry.

The carved poles of the Nass were of better quality than those of the Skeena, but were less numerous, as the Nass people gave up their ancient customs much earlier than the Gitksan, around 1880 or 1890. The technique of pole carving in both areas documents the passage from the earlier and better art of the *Haesem-hliyawn* type, to that of *Hlamee*.

The Tsimshian of the lower Skeena, on the other hand, were never devoted to the art of carving totem poles. A tall slab of stone was erected to commemorate an important historical event. Although the Tsimshian did not adopt the relatively recent custom of erecting carved memorial poles for their dead, they did retain the older custom of painting crest symbols on the front of their houses in native pigments. While no totem poles ever seem to have stood in the village of Gitsees, near the mouth of the Skeena, five house-front paintings were still clearly remembered and described in the late 1920s. Many houses of neighboring tribes were decorated in this style, which at one time may have been fairly common along the coast.

Kwakiutl inside house post at Koskimo.
B.C. Provincial Museum

This remarkable Northwest Coast custom of carving and erecting house poles and tall mortuary columns, or of painting crests on house fronts is sufficiently consistent in style to suggest that it originated in a single center, and spread outward in various directions. The limits of its distribution coincide with those of Northwest Coast art in general, which includes the carving or painting of wood, leather, stone, bone, and ivory.

Northwest Coast art seems much more ancient in some of its smaller forms than in its larger ones. Its origin can be traced back to prehistoric times. Symbolic figures were standardized as early as the times of Spanish, English, and French explorers, between 1775 and 1800. Most of the early circumnavigators — Cook, Dixon, Meares, Vancouver, Marchand, and La Perouse — give ample evidence that masks, chests, and ceremonial objects were, in the late 1800s, decorated in the style now familiar to us. They also mention that house fronts were decorated with painted designs. There is, however, a striking lack of evidence everywhere as to the existence

Modern Kwakiutl inside house posts decorate Thunderbird Park
House in Victoria, B.C.

of totem poles proper or detached memorial columns along the coast. For instance, although Dixon examined several of the Haida villages on the Queen Charlotte Islands, he failed to mention totem or house poles, even though he minutely described small carved trays and spoons.

But there were already, from 1780 to 1800, some carved house posts in existence. Captain Cook observed a few carved posts inside the house of some chiefs at Nootka Sound, where he wintered in 1780, and Webster, his artist, reproduced the features of two or them in his sketches. Meares, in 1788 and 1789, observed Nootka carvings in the same neighborhood, which he described as "Three enormous trees, rudely carved and painted, which formed the rafters, and which were supported at the ends and in the middle by gigantic images, carved out of huge blocks of timber." Elsewhere, he calls them "misshapen figures." The earliest drawing of a carved pole is that of a Haida house frontal or entrance pole, recorded in Bartletts' journal of 1790.

David Hancock

The custom of carving and erecting mortuary columns to honor the dead is therefore modern, or post-Contact. In spite of this, it is not easy to trace its origin to a single birthplace. Even the simple poles of the Nootkas as described by Cook are not likely in themselves to represent a form of native art in its purely aboriginal state, undisturbed by foreign influences. At that time, iron and copper tools were used everywhere by expert craftsmen. The Northwest Coast had been discovered by Russian explorers several decades prior to Cook's arrival, and the Spanish had also left traces of their visits. As well, the influence of the French and English had been felt on the Northwest Coast through contacts with inter-mediate tribes, and with halfbreeds and *coureurs de bois*, who had traveled west of the mountain passes. From our records of exploration, it appears certain that the Northwest Coast people were accessible to foreign influence for more than two hundred years. The natives themselves were highly receptive to foreign influence, displaying skill in acquiring and utilizing those white trade goods which best suited their needs.

Precisely where the totem poles, or mortuary columns, first appeared, and exactly when, are two interesting, though elusive, points. Our evidence eliminates the Gitksan, or the Tsimshian proper, from among the possibilities. Similarly, the tribes farther south cannot be considered. The Bella Bellas were painters rather than carvers. Kwakiutl and Nootka plastic art remained very crude compared with that of the northern tribes. It was seldom used as an illustration of crest figures, as these were of relatively minor importance among the tribes to the south of the Skeena. Totem poles among the Kwakiutl and the Nootka are all very recent; few were erected before 1880. The most familiar of the Kwakiutl poles, those of Alert Bay, were all carved and erected after 1890. None of them had been carved prior to the visit of C.F. Newcombe in that year.

Haida burial post at Skedens Village on Queen Charlotte Islands. The body of the deceased Chief was placed in a box behind the frontal board displaying "Dogfish" crest.

David Hancock

25

At first sight it seems more likely that the Tlingit, of southern Alaska, might have initiated the custom of erecting memorials to the dead. They were closer to the Russian traders, and must have been among the first to obtain iron tools. Although they were the most skillful carvers and weavers, it appears that the credit for originating totem poles is not theirs. Early explorers in some of their villages made no known mention of large carvings, or of house or grave posts similar to those observed among the Haida farther south. From a keen and experienced observer of these people, Lieutenant G.T. Emmons, who was stationed on the Alaskan coast for many years, we learn that the northern half of the Tlingit nation had no totem poles at all until relatively recently. The few poles that were within the scope of his observation were the property of a family or families that originally belonged to the southern tribes, and retained their southern affiliations.

The Haida must also be dismissed from consideration as the possible originators of pole carving. Haida poles, as we know them, are partly house poles proper. House poles are far more common among the Haida than they are among the Tsimshian, constituting a greater percentage of carving. In fact, very few Nass River carvings were house poles. The two large posts observed among the Haida by Bartlett and Marchand between 1788 and 1792 formed the doorways of houses.

Although the Haida villages were often visited at the end of the eighteenth century and in the first part of the nineteenth, we find no other reference to large poles. The famous rows of poles at Massett and Skidegate, photographed about 1880, were an advanced, conventionalized form. Most Haida poles were carved between 1830 and 1880, presumably by carvers who were contemporaries.

The Haida poles were only ten to thirty years old when most Indians became converts to Christianity. As traditional customs were abandoned around 1880, the Haida cut down these poles and sold them to whites. Although there is no evidence of mortuary poles among the Haida prior to 1840 or 1850, a few earlier and transitional ones may have been prototypes of later poles.

Horizontal Tlingit burial pole at Wrangell Alaska.

Field Museum of Natural History, Chicago

Nootka pole from Friendly Cove.
David Hancock

27

It is possible that the totem pole in its conventionalized form originated among the Nisrae or northern Tsimshian of the Nass River. It is evident, from native traditions, that although this form of commemorating the dead was not an ancient custom, it was established here at an earlier date than it was among the Gitksan or the Tsimshian. Haida and Tlingit carvers probably imitated those along the Nass.

The estuary of the Nass River was the most important trade route for eulachon grease, a fairly universal and indispensable staple along the coast. To obtain grease, the Haida, Tlingit, Tsimshian, and Gitksan traveled over the sea or the inland trails every spring and camped in several temporary villages along the lower Nass, trading here for weeks at a time. During these yearly exchanges, cultural features of the local hosts were constantly under the observation of the strangers, and were often a cause for envy or aggression. It is doubtful, on the other hand, that the Tsimshian of

B.C. Provincial Museum

Kwakiutl wolf feast dish — not dissimilar to horizontal mortuary poles.

Haida argillite miniature poles. These truncate poles were specifically carved as a tourist trade item — even last century.

the Nass ever traveled to the Queen Charlotte Islands or the Tlingit country, except briefly to make a raid or an occasional visit to relatives. The resemblance of Tlingit poles to the earlier poles from the Nass River area supports the conclusion that free-standing poles were first carved by Tsimshian artists.

Evidence abundantly shows that the Nass River tribes made totem poles at an earlier period than the upper Skeena people. Several of the Gitwinlkul villagers had hunting grounds on the upper Nass, and the Gitksan used to travel every spring to the lower Nass for eulachon fishing, or to trade pelts or dried fruit cakes with the coast tribes. In the course of time, a strong cultural influence from the more progressive tribes of the coast thus resulted.

The Nass River carvers were, on the whole, the best on the Northwest Coast. Their art reached the highest point of development ever attained in the region. Their totem poles were the finest and among the tallest seen anywhere.

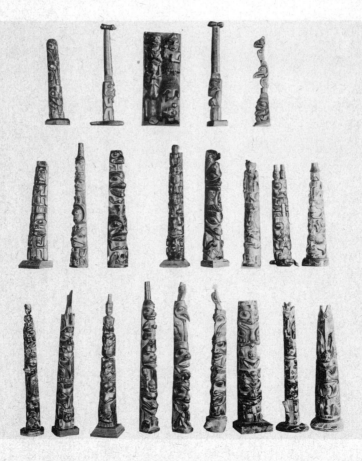

Field Museum of Natural History, Chicago

New Tongas, Alaska.

Field Museum of Natural History, Chicago

31

Tlingit memorial pole at Saxman Alaska.
National Museum of Canada

Modern Tlingit pole erected in Seattle WA.
David Hancock

33

Tlingit maiden with woodworm at Klawak, Alaska.
National Museum of Canada

34

Chief Shakes' house at Fort Wrangell, Alaska.
National Museum of Canada

National Museum of Canada

Fine Tlingit longhouse with traditional entrance through hole in house frontal pole.

Kitwanga village after poles were re-erected.
National Museum of Canada

Inside Tsimshian longhouse showing inside house posts supporting main roof beams. Kitwanga Village, B.C.
National Museum of Canada

New Ksan Village, near Hazelton, B.C. →
National Museum of Canada

39

Kitwancool pole that was re-erected beside a new house. Originally entry was through the oval hole which was lower when pole was buried.

Donovan Clemson

Collection of poles at Tsimshian village of Gitarhdanks.

National Museum of Canada

HAIDA

Haida poles. Above a reconstruction in Vancouver, B.C.

Stanley Park. At right Anthony Island.
David Hancock

44

FRONT OF CHIEF'S HOU

Bella Coola mortuary pole above and monument pole at right.
David Hancock

Haida house at Massett, Queen Charlotte Is.
National Museum of Canada

A Bella Coola inside house post.

Bella Coola longhouses with house frontal poles.

Kwakiutl poles at Alert Bay above and Stanley Park, Vancouver, B.C.
David Hancock

Kwakiutl ceremony showing inside
house posts.

Kwakiutl inside house post.

National Museum of Canada

Early view of Alert Bay.
B.C. Archives

Nootka longhouse depicted by early artist.

Nootka pole.
David Hancock

Captain Jack's famous inside house posts at Friendly Cove, B.C.

National Museum of Canada

Nootka memorial pole with close-up of Sun Crest.

David Hancock

Modern Coast Salish poles at Duncan, B.C.
David Hancock

Coast Salish Chiefs grave.

Coast Salish grave figure at Patricia
Bay, B.C.

Coast Salish longhouse at Quamichon,
B.C.

National Museum of Canada

National Museum of Canada

63